Footprints in Sand

Also by William Cotter and published by Ginninderra Press

Poetry
The Darkness of Swans
The White Blood of Moonlight
Cloud Gazing
Refractions
Light Within the Stone
Pen Points of Light, Shade and Half-light
Mirror: Collected Poems
Of Forms and Shapes (Pocket Poets)
Budj Bim (Picaro Poets)
Betka (Picaro Poets)

Fiction
Thoughts By a Window
Storm Over Bakery Hill

Play for voices
Of Baiame and a Tree That Said, 'Dig'

William Cotter

Footprints in Sand

Footprints in Sand
ISBN 978 1 76109 470 5
Copyright © text William Cotter 2023
Cover image: W. Sabine from pixabay

First published 2023 by
GINNINDERRA PRESS
PO Box 3461 Port Adelaide 5015
www.ginninderrapress.com.au

Contents

The Moment Caught	9
Black Girl Alone in the Street	10
Budj Bim	11
Deen Maar	12
Eels	13
Juvenile Justice	14
Lake Mungo at Night	15
Reconciliation	17
Song of the Fragmites	18
The Maker of Fire	19
The Stony Rises, Western Victoria	21
Uluru	23
Black Cockatoos in Summer	24
Albatross	25
Coming of the Swans	26
Going of the Swans	27
Coming on a Frosty Night	28
Dawn Over the Snowy River	29
Song of the Lyrebird	30
Straw-necked Ibises	31
The Lyrebird	32
The River Red Gum	33
Track of Light	34
Voice of the Sea	35
Voice of the Lonely	36
Wreck of the *Admella*	37
Wally, the Working Wombat	38
Dawn Through the Charred Forest	39
Drought and the Creek	40
The End of Drought	41

The Deserted Hut	42
The Hammerhead Country	44
Forest	45
New Year's Eve	46
Highway	47
Aftermath of the Fires	48
Revisiting Mallacoota	49
The Moon, the River and the Fox	51
The Quarry	52
Breakfast With the Truckies	53
Bridge	54
Clearing the Land	56
Climate Change	57
Fireside Thoughts	58
Hay Carting	59
Gabo Island	61
In the William Creek Hotel	62
Of Children and Sand	64
Morning Light	66
Beyond Palliative Care	67
A Winter Bloom	68
Lorikeets	69
The Black Cormorant	70
An Almost Ordinary Saturday Morning	71
Lockdown	72
The End of Lockdown	73
First Sighting	74
An Attempted Escape	75
The *Earl Cornwallis*	76
The Death of Charlie Gray	77
Return of Burke, Wills and King to Copper Creek	78
Storm Over the Desert	80

The Ghost and the Billabong	81
The Navvy – Pushing North For 'The Alice'	83
Relic From the Gold Rush	85
A Winter School Day	86
The Blacksmith	87
The Seaman and the Lighthouse	88
My Father's Clock	89
Revisiting an Old Wimmera Home	90
Road Train Seen at Night – Southern Queensland	91
Sputnik	92
The Black Arrow: William Creek	93
The Farmer	94
Visiting a Remembered Woolshed	96
The Circus Tent	97
The Kitchen and the Summer Storm	99
Portland: Not as I Knew it	100
The Droplet	101

The Moment Caught

The poem is the moment living,
The caught-on-radar consciousness
Of its coming and its going,

The moment is the present,
The present the poem,
The poem the ray of light
Held briefly on the hill.

Black Girl Alone in the Street

She shuns the light, seeking the shelter
Of shadows. Banks, shops and offices
Blink in the afternoon sun and around her
The shoppers and the day's commuters
Process. Some may notice her grubby dress,
Some her skinny, black legs, her unkempt, wiry hair,
One or two her unwashed feet, her arms that press
Against her chest. Others may stare,
Feigning sympathy and shaking their heads.
Some may notice her small, crab-like hands
And the battered case they hold. High-spirited
Girls will pass, bright as flowers fanned
By admiring glances.
Some may question how a child of seven
Can be left to wander the streets alone.
Some, as the case bursts open
And cakes of soap, white as polished bone,
Come tumbling down, may feel a slight unease,
Seeing, against this pitiless white,
Her fingers trembling like strips of anthracite.

Budj Bim

The Budj Bim Heritage Landscape, in south-west Victoria, is now a UNESCO World Heritage Site.

Dusk is reddening the scoria rims
And the weeping she-oaks, near the summit,
Stand on guard, warning, through their antique limbs,
That, among his peers, only the chief law man is fit,
To stand here, on the shores
Of the Milky Way, gaze up and retrace,
Through the long, glittering corridors,
The journeys of those who had made this place.

But no wise man remains to stand here now.
Above the silver tremors in the lake,
The white washed moon glides, silent and low.
The monologue of guns, the parents' heartbreak,
The children hunted and felled like frantic,
Fleeing kangaroos, are gone, now, all gone,

And we stand, with only the beautiful, magic
Ocean of stars and the sad, drifting moon.

Deen Maar

Lady Julia Percy Island

Dawn brought shallow half-light over the sea
And Deen Maar, glimpsed and ghosted
On the rim of the world,
Shouldered a heavy, grey mist.
Wind stuffed the afternoon with cloud,
Lightning spattered the sea with brief bursts of yellow,
Thunder bellowed, rain fell
And on the shelves of rock,
Sea lions glared and slid away.
But when dusk swept the sky clear
And the first stars bobbed up,
Deen Maar joined the moon
And together they rose,

A single column of light
On the rim of the world.

Eels

Darlot Creek – For thousands of years the Gunditjmara people of south-west Victoria harvested short finned eels and lived in permanent settlements along Budj Bim's wetlands.

They begin as splinters of light,
So small you can see right through them.
But from the ocean, with all its ups and downs,
They emerge, transformed.

Their heads are small and sharp as spear points,
Their mouths large and set,
Their tubular bodies flexible as rubber tubing

And now, easing through pulsing, clear water,
Parting the waving tentacles of weeds,
Shimmering with the sun above them,
Or sinking into the semi-shade,
They are coming up Darlot Creek
Long, loose lines of them,
Mysterious,
But always coming.

Juvenile Justice

Beneath the patched sky and the tight, rattling sails,
The officer's voice carries the rusty authority of the centuries.
'Well, if you hadn't done anything,
You wouldn't be 'ere, lad, would you?'
And the answer comes in clanking chains,
Heaving decks, foul bunks and fears of Botany Bay.

Even in the harsh Australian sun Yorkshire backs are tough.
But the guard knows his trade. The lash sings, high and insistent.
The body rebels, sinks and silence settles.

Behind the white, intimidating police van
Country and family are swallowed by dust
And fears of whatever lurks ahead.
'Well, lad, if you and your black mates 'adn't done anythin'
You'd still be at 'ome, wouldn't you?'

Well-manicured hands point to the columns and figures.
'Situation's getting worse for these Abo kids.
You'd think once here would be enough, wouldn't you?
Never learn, some of them.'

A black boy is strapped to a chair,
Hooded, left with the sickly smell of urine,
The stabbing voices of derision
And, presumably, a lesson.
But what has he learned?

And how far have we come?

And we can well wonder
How far we have come.

Lake Mungo at Night

Lake Mungo, an ancient, dry lake in the central-west of NSW, is part of the Willandra Lakes system.

You stand mid-centre of the grey divide,
That slow, inevitable slide of light towards dark.
The moon, comfortable and unhurried,
Gives the sculpted dunes their required sheen,
Shrugs aside a few pretend clouds
And launches its long, leisurely stroll between the stars.
Determined to blaze a trail east to west,
A jet plane furrows the grey sky.
But soon it is just another chink of light,
A ripple spending itself,
A memory
And now nothing.

All is calm: the dry bed of the lake,
The head high eucalypts weathered by the daytime wind,
All are silent.

Long gone are the giant kangaroos
And the cow clumsy diprotodons.
Only fragments of bone remain,
Calligraphic minuscules buried in the sand,

Gone, too, are the reeds and the rhythmic waters,
The velvet boys testosterone fuelled,
Pelting their todays towards tomorrows
And the girls, dancing knee-deep in green,

Silent, now, all of them.

But you played like them, once,
Stood on tiptoes to snatch each moment
And felt your breath shimmering with every dawn.

Now, in this slow, descending darkness,
You sense Time spilling its sand through your bones.

But look! Listen!
The shambling stars,
The freshly polished moon
And the wonder of this ancient place beckon still
And the slow, strolling breezes still bear the voices
Oh those ancient people.

Reconciliation

I saw them there, the three black cockatoos,
Comfortable above the ancient eel traps
And gnawing among the wattles.
And I saw and heard the willy wagtail,
A flicker of black and white,
Fluting between the comings and goings
Of light and shade,
Now on the stalk of a reed,
Now on the remnant of a scoria wall
And, all the while, the notes
Were like floating ribbons,
Free in the sunlight.

But, seeing me, he suddenly stopped,
Put down his flute and began to speak.
'Let us talk, together, you and I,' he said.
'Not from loneliness. Not from guilt.
Nor from the pickings of the past.
Rather let us meet, free-flying in the sun.'
Then, fluting again, he rose,
Looking down, as if waiting
And, with him, the black cockatoos,
Free, all of them,
Free in the afternoon light

And around me,
It was as if stone, water and bushland
Were patiently waiting, too.

Song of the Fragmites

Tyrendarra Lava Flow

I heard the reeds singing
And whispering softly together,
Softly and sweetly,
Softly and sweetly together

And I heard the breeze
In the gathering, greying dusk,
Quietly, cautiously, stroking the stalks,
Quietly, cautiously, stroking the stalks

And, then, all was still,
Silent as she shadows sliding past,
Silent as the shadows sliding past.

So, I called to the reeds,
There, with the shadows around me.
'Oh, songsters, sing. Sing again.
Let the breeze bend and move you,
Bend and move you
As you sing.'

And then, as if in answer,
Sweet as water running over stones,
Sweet as water running over stones,
There it came again,
The breeze and the reeds singing together,
Softly and sweetly together.

Then, the darkness fell
And all was still.

The Maker of Fire

They sit together, grandfather, grandson,
Comfortable on the sand,
Hearing the desert whispering
And watching the moon gliding with secrets
The boy is eager to understand.
He knows about the fearsome magic of fire.
He has heard the dry-stone clatter of thunder.
He has seen the yellow spears hurled from the clouds
Piercing the heart of a tree
And exploding into golden, minute stars.

But, tonight, bent, with hands as old as tree roots,
His grandfather, serious and remote,
And using nothing more than a piece of pointed wood
Buried in a pile of kangaroo dung and dry leaves,
Is endeavouring to create magic of his own.
His hands turn slowly at first,
Then faster, faster, the wood bites deeper, deeper

And the boy creeps closer, closer.

Now, thin slivers of smoke,
Grey black between the old man's hands, filter up
And he bends lower, blows gently.
The boy, trembling with excitement, kneels, closer.
From the acrid-smelling pile, flowers open out,
Bright as the cupped red of the desert pea
His mother has often plucked from the shadows and shown him.

Two faces are joined in a gentle, shifting light.
Twigs are added
And the light becomes a small island.

Amazed that his grandfather,
Old as the trees clinging to the river bank,
Can perform such magic,
The boy creeps closer again,
Takes the old man's hand
And together they watch the minute stars
As they circle and lose themselves in the Milky Way

Now, without a word, his grandfather stands up,
Points to the sky

And gives the boy the magic wand.
It sits in his hand.
On it, with the moon cold along its length,
A single spark settles,
Blinks, drifts, away,
Dies
And the old man nods again.

The Stony Rises, Western Victoria

Seen from an express train

Much seems to be little changed,
After these forty years.
Passengers still seek ways to maintain their distance.
Knitters still focus on each stitch.
The young hold paper cups of sweet-smelling coffee.
Some of the oldies hide behind newspapers
And rustle them, occasionally as a warning.
As then,
We hear the tidal rumble of two diesel locomotives
And the anaesthetising beat of metal wheels on metal tracks.

Now I see again those grey volcanic cones cloaked in mist and memory,
The long-dead trunks half hidden beneath lichens and ferns.

In the rushing landscape I glimpse the same abandoned farmhouse,
Cold and lonely among its scrawny pine trees
And I follow the miles of antique dry-stone fences
That struggle even today to keep what is tamed from what is wild.

Fantasies flash past of ghosts among basalt rocks.
Cold hands hold cold metal weapons,
Cold hands hold cold wooden spears
And the stones and wiry grasses are stained with blood.

Now we swing from forest, stone and sunset
Into cleared farmland
And, like characters in a sudden, highlighted scene,
Two boys, both in shorts,
One skinny and white, the other skinny and black,
Are kicking a football near an open gate.
They stop, laugh and wave.
The locomotive answers with a sharp, loud whistle

And we are swept on.

Uluru

Dawn rolls up the spiderwebs,
The half-sketched shapes and the ragged edges.
A peregrine falcon cruises, half throttle,
Through the morning heat
And a flock of finches stream, bright coloured
To a rock pool.
Mirages spread through the afternoon,
Dance, sink and dance again.

Dusk coaxes scarlet from the sandstone walls
And camera toting tourists compete
To capture this special moment.

Night brings the clean plate moon
And, like stones in clear water,
The rippling stars.

But to the Anangu people
They are the Creative Spirits
The Beings that stamped on all things
Rocks, plants, insects, birds, animals,
Humans,
Eternal Life.

Black Cockatoos in Summer

Lake Condah

In the wind sweeping and striking the dry
Cumbungi stalks, it is the black cockatoos
You hear, coming through the afternoon sky
With a promise of clouds heavy with browns and blues
And possum grey rain that will come to cover the lake.

Only now do you see them, the three together,
Loping like purposeful manta rays, sent to unmake
The work of the tight-fisted summer.
The sky is theirs and high above the brown
Reeds in the lake, they shriek, hearing the drum
Of distant thunder. And now, flaring their yellow crowns,
They can lope away, knowing the rain will come.

Albatross

Free to cross the hard-cored moon,
Plough the canvas-heavy clouds
And confront the salt-spiked miles,
He will,
With neither GPS nor compass,
Ride the Roaring Forties round the globe,
Unafraid,
Unsuspecting of the metal fish
Secured to the line lurking
Just below the surface.

Coming of the Swans

Grey with the afternoon's blunt-nosed clouds,
The sky stands knee-deep in the lake,
The rust-iron wind rakes the hills,
Lightning scratches the trees,
Cumbungi clumps bend, straighten
And bend again.
But the swans have come
Sweeping, trumpeting
And now,
As the rain rubs out the day's calligraphy
And the moon is stitched briefly on a patch of clear sky,
They have transformed a pool to a circle of silver.

Going of the Swans

Trumpeting on the high tide of the wind,
They have left our slate-grey lake,
Ready to confront the lightning-spiked storms,
Eager to sail on the streams of sunlight
And print their echoes on the scarlet dusk.

But a stranger will hear their music
And see them sail through streamers of crimson water,
Settle and open, beautiful as dark flowers,
Somewhere on a lake,
As I have done.

Coming on a Frosty Night

In 1952 the Victorian Railways introduced B Class diesel locomotives to the mainline routes within the state, bringing an end to the era of steam.

Only the darkness breathes. Fence posts, silos
And tractors lie, coated in midnight white.
'Will it really come tonight, Uncle John?'
'Come, the Melbourne goods train? Oh, yeah, it'll come.'
The little boy grips the offered hand, smiles,
And the night's spiked silence settles.

Ah! But, now, there is a sound. A something,
Low, distant. And far off, a spider eye
Is winking, parting the thin strings of mist.

The earth itself is rumbling, now;
The light a broom sweeping all things clear.
Bullock nosed, wet and throbbing with purpose,
The new B Class locomotive has come
And a hand, seeming smaller than a moth,
Reaches up to wave.
Brown in the shallow light, a hand waves in response

And the train is gone,
Its splendid blue and gold soon a smudge,
As grey as its cargo.

The little boy climbs back into his uncle's truck,
Smiles, trembles

And the night's spiked silence settles again.

Dawn Over the Snowy River

The sun blinks through the eucalypts,
Stuffs the shadows with crimson rags,
Nudges aside the dish-wash mist
And sidles deep into the gorge.
Bent as paupers on skinny legs,
Wattles release their last gold orbs
And Snowy pines stand in grey-green
Order above the rocks and stumps.

Song of the Lyrebird

Shady Gully

They are gone, now, the flutings,
The magical mimicries,
The risings and falls,
The scales, trills, the multiple calls
With all their marvellous crescendos

And he has gone, too,
Pick, pick, picked his way back into the shadows.

But his music remains, deeper than any thought,
An echo of the joy he had brought.

Straw-necked Ibises

The unkind dismiss us as tip chickens,
Forgetting that beggars can't always choose.
But canny farmers, knowing each season
Unleashes its tiny munchers, will use,
Indeed welcome, our long-billed attention.
Our thousand bare black heads bent to peruse,
Ferret out, swallow all acts of thievery,
Then depart and we do it all for free.

The Lyrebird

Leave the wombat waddling track, the monstrous comedy
Of his burrow and the neat, clinging greenness of his dung.
Skirt the grey kangaroo propped in his gully
And do not provoke the bomb blast of his tail. Among
The tangle of wattles, leave undisturbed the perched wisdom
Of the choughs and the leisurely pen stroke beat of their wings.
Wade through the shallow pools of light and shade. Come
Then, to the grey, moss-edged scaffoldings
Of stone and the organ pipe straightness of 'stringies'.
Listen and you will sense, not hear, the breeze experimenting
On the hung-down leaves and tracing out its future melodies.
Set aside all thought now. Drift through the narrowing
Corridor of light to the semi-dark and you may see him
Slipping like a delicate ghost past a window, his beak and head
Thrust forward, his legs stitching dim,
Meticulous circles of gold and his tail creating in thread
A floating filigree of lace. A blink and he is gone,
A sprite reclaimed by the forest, a memory
Defying word and shape. But wait, now, and listen.

Listen and wait.

There, through the tracery
Of branches, shadow and ferns you hear him. Only he,
He in all the forest, can capture such longing,
Distil with unalloyed simplicity
The essence of its truth and send it forth in such an offering.

The River Red Gum

Geriatric? Yes. Indeed, some say comical,
Claim my half-exposed roots are the sticking through legs of a tramp.
Others, less unkind,
Compare me to a war veteran shipped home
And abandoned here.
But I come from an ancient race,
Defying storms, chiselling sunlight, back-rubbing bullocks
And even those hordes of nibbling beetles.
Yes. My branches do resemble the arms of old men.
My leaves do droop down,
Inconsequential snippets curled at the edges.
But the dry-voiced ravens and gaudy parrots still come,
Seeking shelter, hollows to nest in
And I stand whiter, cleaner than anything else
On any moonlit night.
I do not boast of my journey through the millennia.
I have no great wisdom to impart.
I am not the Tree of Knowledge.
I am not the Tree of Life.
I am simply a tree,
Proud of my history

And hanging on.

Track of Light

Stroking the grey coming-down dusk,
The swan brakes and settles on the lake,
Her trumpeting, in the cold, spiked air, clear as metal struck.

Balanced postcard perfect on the slow circling water,
She gathers the glittering ribbons cast off from the moon
And sails between islands of reeds, creating a trail of silver,

A trail that follows, soft as a strand of pearls
Strung on darkening ruffled velvet
And rippling like a child's flowing curls,

A trail that is a moment's beauty,
The echo of a dying song,
But, for the wanderer, a hived-away memory.

Voice of the Sea

I am the voice you hear
When the waves, weary from travelling,
Come, white falling among rocks
And when the ripples winkle whispers from the sand.
It is my voice you hear
When the breeze, soft as a child's breathing,
Filters through the dunes on moonlit nights
And the ice-tipped wind moans through caves
Deserted even by ghosts.
I am gull cry,
Seal cough
And the brown leather forests of kelp
Rolling and complaining in the shallows.
I am crab scuttle and the pitter patter of children's feet.
The stories of ships skeletonised and rusting.
Ripped sails rattling and whining.
The voice mocking sailors maddened by weeks of calm.
I am the song of mermaids seducing lonely men.
The triumphant suck, blow and bellow from cliffs.
I am the rough-edged, moving mountains.
Moonlight. Starlight
And the sun soft as a blanket.
I am fantasy and truth.
I am the mystery concealed in the shell you hold
Against your ear.
Hold it close and listen.
Listen to the sea.

Voice of the Lonely

I speak of mists and threadbare horizons,
Of scarred and pitted rock, of dish-wash waves,
Lonely gulls and wallowing snakeskin kelp.
I speak of knotted, evil-smelling weed,
Of rough sketched footprints quickly washed away.
Of cliffs and fragile flowers clinging on.
But, most, I speak for the frightened children
Caught on the darkened margins of the world.

Wreck of the *Admella*

On the night of 6 August 1859, the SS *Admella*, a steamer working between Adelaide and Melbourne, crashed into a submerged reef off Carpenter Rocks, south-west of Mount Gambier, in South Australia. Of one hundred and thirteen passengers and crew, only twenty-four survived.

There is no coarse laughter from weary seamen
Bunched below.
No restless shuffling of children in their bunks.
No curse as the cook tosses into the sea
One final pot of rotting fish.
Not tonight,
Only the sickly yellow
Whip-smooth strips of lightning,
The grey smear across Northumberland's light,
The unsteady image of a coastline,
The sea sucking,
The mutter of surf,
Persistent as distant gunfire

And the vessel steaming.

To the sailor, spring taut at his post,
Clutching for reassurance,
The wind whispers,
'Go below, man. Knock out your pipe.
Sink in your dreams to the arms of your woman.
All will be well.'

But, where the long gliding waves curl cold,
The reef is already sharpening its teeth.

Wally, the Working Wombat

Pick and shovel, sand and gravel,
Wally Wombat digs his tunnel.
Plan it, punch it, scrabble it and spread it,
Poke in your arm and I'll quickly scrunch it.

Pick and shovel, sand and gravel,
Wally Wombat digs his tunnel.

Daytime, night-time, I'll upgrade it.
Room for my mate with an inch to spare it.
Snarl at the dogs as I go to dig it,
Scatter all the sheep as they go to market.

Pick and shovel, sand and gravel,
Wally Wombat digs his tunnel.

Sleeves up, head down,
Nose to the grinding stone,
Piling up dirt that will make your blood boil,
Dozing through the winter while you wish you were able.

Hard stuff, soft stuff,
I'll abrade it.

Hold it, hold it! We'll announce it,
Poke in your arm and he'll quickly scrunch it.

Pick and shovel, sand and gravel,
Wally Wombat digs his tunnel.

Dawn Through the Charred Forest

Staining the sea's creased seams
And picking apart the patched shadows
Draped on the dunes, dawn scribbles
On the toppled tea tree stumps,
Scores with scarlet the silver tops
And the gaunt grey gums, then ghosts
With phantom flames the forest and the gullies.

Drought and the Creek

Once purposeful and going somewhere,
This creek, now shrivelled,
Lost between indifference
And the slow, unfolding summer afternoon,
Is going nowhere.
Shadows cling to the hollows
And roots of the trees, taut arteries for decades,
Lie, loose as discarded snakeskins, along the banks.
In the few rust-stained pools, mud congeals and condemns,
Silence snuffs out even the gravelly voice of the crow
And hope has packed up and gone.

The End of Drought

Predictable, this dusk,
This shamble of shade, fence post, gatepost,
The chuddering cough of this tractor
Coming home.

Predicable, too,
The wind suddenly cold,
The lightning, sharp as cracking glass
And the thunder muttering weakly in a corner of the sky.

But not this closer gravelly voice,
This drumming on the roof,
This gnome become a frog,

This joy
Bursting out to meet the rain.

The Deserted Hut

The Flinders Ranges

Dawn dances upon the eyeless skulls of the cattle.
The early sun sidles across the clapped-out country.
The wind teases the weatherboard walls,
Then wanders away to find the afternoon.

Grey as threadbare fabric, dust drifts round the veranda.
Soil that peeled away, once,
Rich and clean from the plough, is gone.
Of the rows of wheat that stood
With their perfect heads bright as trembling prayers,
Only the stalks remain,
Residue from that bare-knuckle stoush
Where Hope lost in a knockout

A few spitballs of mud lie in the bottom of the dam.
Here, where 'roos had scrambled and bellied in search of water,
Cockatoos land briefly, then spiral away,
Stabbing the sky with their high, belligerent shrieks.

Close to the hut a drum rusts.
A fox skin rots on a fence.
A mattress vomits on the porch
And sickly strands of light seep through the roof.

That shaded crucifix held a slaughtered beast, once.
The dog chain still lies, buried in the sand
And from that peppermint branch
A child launched out into the universe,
Sustained in her swing and return by her laughter
And the wings of her billowing dress.

There is here, now,
Only the terrible certainty of defeat.

Yet, on a mound that might have been a sandcastle,
Something has taken root,
A something refusing to surrender its minute dream.
It is Sturt's Desert Pea,
Daring, in spite of all, to open its scarlet, black-centred eyes.

The Hammerhead Country

I drink with conviction, here, in the hammerhead country,
Comb the froth from my beard and mouth,
Nod and leave. One shuns formality.
Those tinsel tinted descriptions from the south
Mean little. Up here in the hammerhead country.

Now, the shingle-back highway disgorges a truck that lurches,
Stops, creaking with cattle. The driver
Bangs the cabin door shut and, startled, a 'wedgie' tractors
Off and settles into an orbit above the cattle. 'Bugger
Of a day,' I venture, with my best outback accent, but get no reply.

In a cascade of flashes and noisy irritation, lorikeets
Spread chaos above the wreck of a stock pen.
Twin toilets stand by a fence, corrugated sheets
Of iron vaguely differentiated, 'MEN' and 'WOMEN'
And glitter in the heat, pathetic as abandoned space junk.

Husks of dust curl round an empty tank. From its edge,
Mumbling its traditional mantra of death, a raven
Preens its cassock, then lifts above a saltbush hedge.
As I drive off, hotel, plain and horizon
Melt into a mud-coloured mirage, drifting, fading and flowing again.

Forest

I see your canopy piercing the sky,
The filtered sunlight
And your elephant-hide stringies.
I see the long-dead trunks covered in creepers
And the patches of moss nestling in the shade.
I see brown, leather tongues of fungi,
Shimmering waves of bracken fern,

And even, just now,
Two lyrebirds scurrying across my path.

I hear the cut short snap of whipbirds,
The wonga pigeon's helicopter whirl
And, in the deep recesses of the gullies
I hear the dry-stone voice of ravens.

I feel the paper dry crackle beneath my boots,
The soft moss against my hands,
The brown corrugations of antique ironbarks
And your breath filtered through the leaves.

Yes, I see, hear and touch all of these.
Sense your great heart steady in its work.

But I fear for your future,
Knowing the mechanised forces that prowl your borders.

New Year's Eve

East Gippsland, 2020

Untroubled, Time trundles on.
The wind dusts off its grey overalls,
Crosses the crimped, dry wetland and stalls,
Briefly, among the spindly melaleucas.
On his usual branch, a magpie practises his cadenzas.
Cleverly disguised as a fantail,
A pint-sized acrobat pirouettes mid-air. Ministerial
In glossy black, three cockatoos lope through our garden.
Delinquent galahs give up trying to fly in unison.
Chooks do their habitual turn, prod and pick.
A pobblebonk frog cranks up his gravelly rhetoric

And the day rolls on.

But what are the pink-grey lines
Spidering out above those pines?

And why is that fresh bridal gown cloud
Drifting now, heavy as an unwashed shroud?

Highway

After the fires, Cann River to Genoa, 27 February 2020

The road is a thin, grey strip,
Strung beneath the chewed horizon
And the broken forest.
On either side,
Dozers plough through a surf of shattered trees.
Mechanical mouths clamp on salvageable logs,
Disgorge them, like coffins, in piles
And log trucks,
Spreading clouds of charred leaves behind them,
Cart them away.
No bird sings.
No black cockatoo
Lopes between the straight or crooked tombstone trees.

But, in a clearing,
Like a ribbed, grey sculpture,
A kangaroo is pricking his ears.
On a dry creek bed,
Tree ferns are dancing,
Defiantly, joyously green on their comical, old man stumps.
On blackened silver tops,
Minute green eruptions catch the afternoon sun
And, already, delicate as lace,
Bracken ferns wave, green and hopeful, in the gullies.

Aftermath of the Fires

Betka Beach, 11 February 2020

The sea lopes towards its usual blue dreaming afternoon.
Clouds unfurl their grey, white sails and form leisurely,
Distant loops. But, strewn along the beach,
Black, spider lines mark the flames' demonic dancing
And, on the clifftops,
Skinny tea trees and banksias are hanging,
Silent in their condemning ugliness.
Branches litter the dunes, smelling
Of wet smoke and tracks have become going-nowhere scratches,
Blistered ashen grey in the clearings.

But, almost unnoticed, two magpies
Pick through the debris, pry
Among the charred, chewed leaves, then rise
Back into the stringy afternoon sky

And, within a shallow circle of light,
A nondescript plant spreads brave, leathery fingers.

Revisiting Mallacoota

Two years after the fires

Oh, yes.
One does not easily file away
Haunting, grey hessian skies,
Lingering coils of smoke,
Rasping sandpaper winds,
Bulldozed trees like the hulls of wrecked boats
Piled beside the highway,
Nor the three burnt 'roos, I saw on four successive days,
Ghost grey, hollow ribbed and clinging to the shadows.
I remember
The clay, brown as cardboard, crackling beneath my boots
Ash, like dirty snow pushed against fence posts,
Trees collapsing in the distance,
The plate-flat moon drifting among chipped stars,
Skeletal branches
And the moaning breeze.
But I did not hear any sounds of birds.
No wing beats. No calls of magpies
Coming clear as water rippling through stones.
No crisp exchanges between pairs of whipbirds
Scrabbling through the undergrowth.

I smelt the ash, the spidering strips of spent smoke
And each day the wind
Carrying the heavily laced, condemning smell of death.

But, now,
Without prologue or fuss,

Nature has buried its fingers in the darkness of the earth.
Green rivulets are sliding into gullies.
Tree ferns and grass trees are rising,
Eager for the sun.
Heath wattles are bursting forth in the clearings,
Gold and spiky green.
Like strips of paper
Pinned on the black branches of 'stringies' and box trees,
Bright, leather leaves are hanging on.

Along the dunes
Tendrils of running postman spill across the grey sand.
Blooms of everlastings reach up.
White correa flowers tremble on long, smooth stems.
Worker bees,
Bulbous, mini miners, covered in gold,
Come and go.
Flirting and chattering,
Moving with the precision of ballerinas,
Fairy wrens skip between the bushes.

I see, hear and smell the Earth waking up.
And, as I explore this corridor of youthful, exuberant green,
I sense the power of this miracle unfolding around us.

The Moon, the River and the Fox

Above the brown, featureless water
The moon clears the melaleucas
And whitewashes the fish scale outcrops of rock.
Slow, silent, the breeze probes the tangled forest
And sidles into the gorge.

The river shepherds the stars into quiet pools,
Slows, widens,
Steers past the rock piles, the shaggy clumps of cumbungi
And breaks through the ragged edges of the mist.

Head and tail low, the fox slides from darkness to semi-light,
His breath sickly and coiling away, his ears pricked and his eyes
Slow burning in the hot blackness of the summer night.
Hated and hunted come dawn,
He does not fear the darkness

And the sun will creep over a postcard gorge, a river,
And, perhaps
The mangled body of a wallaby
Stained in rivulets of red.

The Quarry

I remember, now, seventy years later,
Summer's tide of green grass there on the hillside
And the quarry's lip, crude as an open wound.
Most vividly, I recall the sheer, blue-brown rock face,
To a small child, the dark substance of nightmares
And the chasm that showed man's control,
His power to wrench, haul away, crush
And reduce glittering rocks to splinters
Even a child could hold in his hand.

I recall, too, the explosion shed squatting
Higher up, command centre of dark magic,

Sometimes, the punch in the belly explosions,
The bursting brown dust and the rock collapsing.

But, now, rusty as an antique cubby house,
The crusher stands, forlorn, the roost of pigeons.
And weeds, scratchy, but persistent creep down the cliff face.

Breakfast With the Truckies

Beneath the slow, swirling fans, here,
In the drab, worked-over lounge,
I guess the ritual remains the same.

The rough, tight camaraderie, talk of road conditions,
Estimated times of going and coming,
The tossed in obscenities,
The smokes jagged into ash trays
And the standard shorts, the boots, the singlet,
The thrown-back cap or the slouch hat.

The eyes never far from these road trains
That slouch, big as islands in the shade,
Silent with purpose
And crowned with belligerent bull bars
Set to throw aside any careless 'roos
On the spidering, dusty roads to the south.

Beyond them, I see the scrubland of cranes on the wharf,
The boys fishing on the end of laughter,
More intent on their cigarettes,
A runabout worrying the early sea

And a single ore carrier, lean and clean as a swept street,
Sliding slowly seawards,
Nudged by six blunt-nosed, pugnacious tugs.

Noticing my interest, a truckie looks up.
'The *Confidence*. Loaded with ore. Headin' for Japan.'
I want to know more.
But chairs grate. Cigarettes are punched into ashtrays.
Bodies straightened
And the truckies are gone.

Bridge

It is seventy years since I stood on this bridge,
Watching the creek run its brown-stained fingers
Over the scribbles of bird droppings
And moss on the pylons,
Then shrug its shoulders
And ramble on
But the memories have come,
Insinuating themselves into the summer dusk.

Below, their carapace little capsules of fire,
Frantic boatmen still follow their rituals,
Their zigzag crossings.
But the years have taken their toll
And their hieroglyphics are foreign to me, now.

I stood here with the kids I knew as mates,
Threw stones and counted the explosions
As they shattered the water,
Worried passing water rats,
Destroyed with a volley Nazi landing craft
And heaved in logs in winter that spun away
Like bloated pigs.

Once I saw this bridge
Locked for days in the arms of a flood,
Then hurled aside
As if the creek had suddenly gone mad.
It lay, naked as a stranded whale
And I saw the workers flense away its flesh
And heard the eel-smooth 'monkey'
Drive in new piles, late into the night
And the hammering and reshaping
Going on for many weeks.

Now, by the farmhouse overlooking the creek,
A truck shudders into life,
Throws out its milky smear of light and heads for the bridge.

I look down once more,
Release my memories to the night

And sense the water and time sliding irrevocably away.

Clearing the Land

The tangled shadows loop through the forest
And his body urges him to stop.
But he tenses, readies again
And his axe swings, explodes against the trunk.
He straightens, sees the pencil-thin line of blood on his hand,
The brown blood seeping from the wounded trunk
And he hears the echo swallowed by the forest.
The dirty grey of dusk hardens into darkness.
But he must continue,
Swinging, striking, suppressing pain,
Until, at last, he hears the wrenching,
The groaning and the 'stringy', like a stranded ship,
Comes crashing down.
Tomorrow's work lies crumpled before him
And he straightens, feels the quickened pain in his back,
The hostility of the forest around him
And, perhaps, a cold sense of triumph.

Climate Change

Black swans are tracing their purposeful line
Through the evening's maze of scarlet air
And below them, the tendrils of dusk twine
Through the foul, rusting water. There,
Swamp hens square off, as always raucous,
Ducklings struggle across plasticine clay
And scraggy, hook-billed straw-necked ibises
Pick and forage in search of careless prey.

A whistling kite props, tilts and plunges down
Into the reeds, while, high and untroubled,
A wedge-tailed eagle cruises on, alone,
Keeper of the skies surrounding his world.

But, on the bank, bloated fish rot, obscene
As battered carcasses of submarines.

Fireside Thoughts

by the Deddick River, June 2018

Logs, snugged one upon the other,
Breathe quietly and whisper.
Scribbles of smoke, fine as lace,
Drift above the flannel-grey ash in the fireplace
And snippets of memories, elusive as butterflies,
Drift and silently rise: times alone,
With stars sharp and white as bone,
Times with my laughing children
And the autumn campfire our warming companion,
Times, when, alone again, smoke and flame
Bore their cargo of remembered guilt and shame.

Somewhere, a gunshot rings out.
Somewhere, an animal falls.
Someone shouts
And the night, with no sign of hurrying,
Restores the silence, spreading its grey-veined wings.

Hay Carting

'Yeah, fewer bales. Lighter this year, too.'
There is no change in the procedure, of course.
The Bedford, slightly more arthritic,
Coughs, lurches and stops by the hay shed.
The truck door grates and slams.
The boss stands, rock solid on the tray
And I, like a monkey, scramble up to await the next bale,
Hoping I don't unwittingly stir a brown snake
From its customary siesta in the afternoon sun.
Seeds and dust splutter out into the shed
As each bale comes to settle,
Comfortable as a drunk among its fellows.

Yes. No real change.
Except, that is, for the voice. It is sharper,
More resigned than last year.
'Yeah. Look. Nearly toss this bugger up one hand.'
His mouth snaps like a trap
And I nudge the offending bale into place,
Wincing as the stalks scratch my bare arms.

Finally, the afternoon hardens,
The iron roof mutters, cracks its aching joints,
The spotless sky bends westward
And the last bale totters up to me.

I hear, with relief, 'Yeah, that'll do us.
Another season done. Not so good, though.
Could be a bugger of a year comin' up.'
I nod.
The truck door grates, slams

And the Bedford lurches out from the shed.

Gabo Island

Gabo Island sits about sixteen kilometres from Mallacoota and five hundred metres from the mainland. The lighthouse was constructed between 1858 and 1862, using pink, local granite. It is the second highest in Australia.

A fishing boat plods through the open sea,
Its hull red stained by the setting sun
And its single spiderweb light slowly
Swinging from its mast. Spun
High by the wind, in clean, grey and white,
Gulls follow their winding track homeward
And, coming silent as a ghost, twilight,
Broad as unrolling carpet, sweeps unheralded
Across the water.

Now, a cold, single star gleams over Gabo
And the plate-scoured moon tilts over Tullaberga.
They share the unbridled southern ocean's flow.
But they are doomed to be apart, forever.
They are punished lovers, grieving in stony silence,
Or lamenting in a voice no more than a whisper.

In the William Creek Hotel

William Creek, on the Oodnadatta Track, fronts the enormous
Simpson Desert. It has a permanent population of ten!

He sits, the seasoned drinker,
Sixty years of redness and beer
Propped on a stool.

'Bugger of a country, this is.
Kick you in the guts, it will.'

I notice the shingle-back highway disgorging a truck
In front of the pub
And hear the cattle
Lurch like a heap of drunks as it stops.

'Take those Krauts, now. Took off for Lake Eyre,
They did. Years ago, it was. Poor devils.
Mad drivin' their van out on the salt. Bloody mad.
Mighta looked all right;
Like me wife's pastry – crisp on top.
But bogged to the guts, she was.

And ya sort of feel sorry for 'em, don't ya?'
Heat like a sheet of iron and the Lake white,
Burnin' the eyes
And not a soul to help 'em?

Been there meself, once, in summer.
Only once. At night you can hear the silence,
Strange whisperin's between the Lake and the sky
And the moonlight clean as a knife.
Heard a dingo there, too. Like a mad woman it was.
Made me blood freeze, that did.'

In a cascade of colour, sparks and noise outside,
Lorikeets burst from a rusty tank

And the driver muscles in beside me.

'And must have driven them Germans mad, too,
Watchin' the sun and the night,
With their van stranded like a bloody boat,
Stuck to the axles.
Poor devils.
Took off, she did. Headin' for 'ere, William Creek.
No chance,
Runnin', then walkin'
And droppin' and dyin' by the track.
Bloke stayed by the van and he survived.'

The driver orders a beer
And a 'wedgie' swivels its lethal head, low above the truck.

'Yeah, bugger of a country, eh, Jack?'
There is a nod above the white flower of froth.

'Kick you in the guts, it will.'

And it does:
Fists of sharp-edged wind and heat
As I escape to the Toyota,
Switching on the engine and the air conditioner
With unashamed relief.

Of Children and Sand

        on a beach
                and running from us

Teasing the white knife edge of the tide,
They are free of us, now

She, on stumpy, copper legs,
With her yellow dress spread wide
And her long black hair trailing behind,
A mini kaleidoscope of colour,
He, with his bare feet, black shorts and white T-shirt,
An angular, running penguin

And both rolling their laugher ahead

And both weaving a web of laughter.

They are Adam and Eve
Free in the garden before the Fall
And their joined hands propel them forward,
On and unashamed through the glories of their innocence.

Our clumsy, dinosaur prints lie
Grey as concrete in the troubled sand above the waterline.
The prints of their feet are the corners of stars,
Gone in an instant
And re-established, briefly, further on.

We see the risks,
The vexed, threatening sky
Split like a curtain through which the rain might pour,
The distant *Spirit of Tasmania*
Tethered to Prince's Pier,
The solid block of flats
And the swinging, anchored cranes on the wharfs.

For them
The Bay is perpetual light,
Their only connection with the Earth
The washed-smooth sand
And the water thrown up like sparks by their feet.

Morning Light

Dawn runs its fingers through the gorge.
Wattles rub the sleep from their eyes,
Knobbly-kneed eucalypts rush to appear presentable.
The sloping forest buries its hands in the morning sun,
Stops, drinks, expands.
Cliffs harden into reflective walls
And the river,
Having tested its muscles in the morning light,
Nods in approval
And wanders on.

Beyond Palliative Care

They come together, the oncologist and the palliative nurse.
He solid and middle-aged. She slim, almost delicate
And the old man wonders why one so desirable, so youthful,
Should subject herself, each day,
To rows of thin, mechanical stands, blinking dials, swirling chemical smells,
Drawn, shadow faces
And why today, as every day,
She stands, statuesque at the end of his bed,
Clutching the obligatory green folder.
A firm handshake from the specialist. A smile at his wife
And the expected words, modulated, professional, but almost gentle.
'I am sorry, John. There is no more we can do.'
A pause. 'And I think, I think we all knew that.'
Another pause. A brief hiatus quickly filled.
'But our staff are well trained. They will ensure your comfort.'
A head unexpectedly bowed.
The sense of professionalism struggling and painfully re-established.
A final handshake. A smile at his seated wife
And he is gone. Back into the sunlight.

The nurse comes forward, checks the impressive dials
And her eyes, so bewitching in the previous months,
Are now as soft as his daughter's, brown, thoughtful, almost sad
And, for the first time, the old man wants to weep.

Finally they are alone, husband and wife.
Above them masterpieces of medicine stand out clearly.
But, when the sun finally flushes through the ward,
It settles on four imperfect hands joined as one
And two faces close together.

A Winter Bloom

Shadows stain the spindly melaleucas,
Swans stitch circles on the lake
And a raucous swamp hen crash lands among the reeds.

In a corner of our garden a single rose bush spiders up
And the winter sun's bony fingers reach one last red bloom.
The whispering scent brings memories of my sister's wedding
Fifty years ago,
My father's funeral
And scarlet petals loosely falling.

I reach up.
But, at the slightest touch,
Scarlet tears, loosely falling,
Drift down to the uncut lawn.

Lorikeets

They are the cheeky front of house comedians,
The flamboyant gymnasts hanging head down,
The principal stars of the high trapeze
Who scorn both safety harness and net,
Loop in gaudy capes of red, blue and gold

And always ready, requested or not,
To cartwheel in concert and do it all again.

The Black Cormorant

With his wings dark as any crucifix
And his neck and needle head turned to the sea,
He is a chiselled extension of the rock he sits on.

Now, silent as a shark,
He is the ghost parting the salt-spiked air

And now,
The lethal, smooth-skinned torpedo
Tracking a careless fish.

An Almost Ordinary Saturday Morning

The village yawns,
Settles into its slow, wake-up routine.
Autumn leaves drift and rub across the lawn
And the sun inches out from the trees.

Toddlers, already energetic as mini tugboats,
Nudge grandparents along the street.
Two boys, up and about early,
Are at work teasing a passing girl.
A young man reaches up from his wheelchair,
Straining to post a letter.

Well-dressed magpies are purposefully pursuing worms.
Ragamuffin sparrows are squabbling on a park bench
And a black, leather-smooth cat
Slinks out from a corner, stops, looks,
Before slouching off.

On the hotel roof
A satellite dish harvests news of little interest,
Spreads it through the half empty bar

And, seated at his post,
The barman mechanically opens the paper,
Flicks from the sports page
To something called the coronavirus,
Scans the headline,
Skips back to news of the cancelled races,
Confines the paper to the rubbish bin

And the village continues its slow, wake-up routine.

Lockdown

Melbourne, July 2020

Gone are the drumming feet,
The tangled conversations
And the tidal comings and goings of trams and cars.
Now, in the grey, untidy dusk,
You hear the swish of a skirt,
The anxious stab of high-heel shoes
And, perhaps, a bell-cold siren.
Doves still circle the spire of Saint Paul's
And settle among the gargoyles.
But the cranes perched above construction sites
Now hang, grey as desiccated spiders
And the CBD lies, almost deserted.
In a park where children came catapulting,
Butterfly bright in the mornings,
A raven preens its feathers,
Snatches discarded scraps of food, lopes away
And the first month of lockdown shrugs its shoulders,
Steadies to begin the next
And an enemy, too small even to see,
Continues to besiege the city.

The End of Lockdown

Melbourne, November 2020

Through early, scribbled sunlight
Satchelled businessmen, shopkeepers
And perfectly coiffured secretaries
Move with purpose,
But maintain their social distance.
Avoiding collisions,
Skate-boarding boys roll between shade, light
And back again.
Unwrapping their lockdown stories,
Schoolgirls bunch at a corner.
Trams, green as articulated caterpillars,
Jostle as they have always done.
Buses and taxis pick up where they had left off

And the CBD, like an old man stirring from uneasy sleep,
Quickens to catch up.

First Sighting

Hard-crusted and doggedly loyal,
This morning, in the salt-sharpened air,
Beneath the whip and creak of sails
Lieutenant Zachary Hicks stood on deck,
His task to winkle out any sign of land
And wake his captain.
Once, crab crawling mists and bursting sunlight
Might have stirred him.
But pain and the dry rattle in his throat
Had rasped his senses.
Yet, that distant, pencil-thin smudge was not mist
And, as it broke, rough-edged but solid, into his consciousness,
He felt his fingers tighten on the cold, rough railing
And a voice, he recognised, with surprise, as his,
Shouted, 'Land, ho! Land ahead!'
Slowly, the gap between sky and sea was filled
With cliffs, tangled trees and clumps of resilient green.
Again, the cry rang out. 'Land, land ho! Land ahead!'
Now, like an actor called to the stage,
James Cook emerged

And soon the sprawling, gritty land would be British.

An Attempted Escape

Between 1788 and 1868, about one hundred and sixty-two thousand convicts were shipped to the Australian colonies from Britain and Ireland. One of the most notorious prisons was built in the 1830s at Port Arthur, about ninety-seven kilometres from Hobart.

I slunk from black to grey and black again.
Smelt the gum leaves. Felt the wet ground
Friendly beneath me feet and heard the breezes,
Even the mopoke cryin' in the hills.
Yes. Like a ghost I was.
But they found me,
Them and their dogs.
Now, in this stone-walled darkness,
I see nothing. I hear me breath and chains
That clank when I move. I smell me sweat
And feel it slitherin' cold down me back.

Soon, now, these high up bars will run with red.
But no redder than my skin, when the lash
Comes to bite and show the worthy King George
That all is settled once more with his world.

The *Earl Cornwallis*

Between 1788 and 1840, twelve thousand women were transported, usually for minor offences, to New South Wales.

Oh, what is that coming so slowly,
So sadly, there, through the mist
And what is that sound I hear
Like sobbing through graveyard stones?

Why, that is the *Earl Cornwallis*, my son
And what you hear are the cries of Ireland's women.

But what are the horrors that bore so deep
That women must stand, like cattle, in chains?
Or, what have they said or done, to deserve such shame?

They have pilfered from purses, my son,
Or marched in the streets for the poor.

And what of that shadow,
That spider thin ghost by the mast?

Why, that is your sister, my son,
Stolen, taken for ever,
So the land and the King may rest in peace.

The Death of Charlie Gray

Probably, of all the exploration expeditions in Australia, the best known is the tragic attempt by Robert O'Hara Burke and his party, in 1861, to reach the Gulf of Carpentaria and return to Melbourne. Charlie Gray was one of the members.

Walk, you say, Mr Robert O'Hara Burke?
Of course I'm walkin', damn you.
Trippin' along on a summer's day
With the wind like heat
Spat out from a blacksmith forge
And you ask if I'm goin' mad? Of course I am.
We're all mad. Blistered. Starvin' like this. And still goin' on.
Let the desert suck us dry, I say.
Loose our bones to wander with the ghost of Leichhardt's man,
The one standin' and grinnin' there among the stones.
You can see 'im there, can't you,
Strokin' 'is beard
And laughin' as the sand trickles through his ribs?
Wait there, ghost of Leichhardt's man. It's Charlie Gray,
Seaman Charlie Gray
Who rolled, cursed and tossed on every rotten ocean
And I'm askin' if the dunes ticklin' your ribs
Are like the waves I knew before madness brought me 'ere.
It's Charlie Gray, soon to die
And 'e wants an honest answer.
Speak damn you.

Walkin'. Walkin'. All on a summer's day.
Walkin' slow on a summer's day.
Slow. Slow on a summer's day.
Walkin', slowly walkin'
And dyin' as 'e walks.'

Return of Burke, Wills and King to Copper Creek

21 April 1861

So, it's ten miles, now, the Gulf to Cooper Creek,
Ten miles, now, for Burke, Wills, King and the ghost of Charlie Gray.

Nine miles, now
And, gored by the barbed-wire sun,
The snake-smooth roots and shingleback stones,
They count, in their staggering,
Step after step,
Boot after boot.

Six miles, now,
For Burke, Wills, King
And the trailing ghost of Charlie Gray.

Four miles, now,
With the smell of rotting 'roos beside them
And the slithering rivulets of make-believe water ahead.

Now two,
And, with the saw-tooth horizon hardening into trees,
There come the first, thin whisperings of hope,
Food, fire shared with their mates
And escape to the south.

Now, one.
Above the intoxicating smell of mud and brown, still water,
They can hear the tangled shrieks of cockatoos
And the earthy mutterings of crows

And, now, they stand, Burke, Wills, King and Gray,
Dust-smeared ghosts together,
Silent, as a dingo sidles away from the deserted camp
And a lingering sliver of smoke creeps out over Cooper Creek.

Storm Over the Desert

Dawn nudges the darkness aside
And a thick light slowly fills the gullies.
Clouds and thunder come, tramping together.
Lightning spurts in pasty yellow.
Afternoon rain creates mini craters smelling of mud.
A feral bull camel chews its cud,
Unconcerned
And a grey kangaroo stands, statue-still,
By a rock.

Now, dusk wipes the sky clear.
The moon rises, clean as a washed plate.
A burrowing frog, patient for many months,
Blinks, licks the mud, lumbers up.

The camel chews on
And the kangaroo lopes leisurely away.

The Ghost and the Billabong

The true story of 'Waltzing Matilda'

Now, let us be clear.
No swaggie's ghost glides around the billabong, scarin' tourists.
The billabong's real, though.
Been there meself. Black as Bushell's tea, it is.
But somehow survives summer and winter. 'Roos love it, of course.
Camped there, too, I have. Under the same red gum, he did, I'm told.
Grand old warrior, that tree. Plenty of fence posts in it,
My farming brother-in-law says. But he's retired, now,
So perhaps the tree is safe.
I've 'eard strange things, there, too.
Squawkin' possums plunging tree to tree.
Even, the bunyip, one night, scrabblin' through the scrub
And howlin', fit to kill in the hills.
Didn't see 'im, though.
And what about that thievin' swaggie? you are about to ask.
Still lives, according to me mate,
The bloke I 'ave a few beers with every Friday.
Was chased by the troopers. Did jump into the billabong.
But crab walked along the bottom, according to me mate.
Scrambled out and scuttled off into the scrub.
Troopers thought he had drowned, of course.
Couldn't have been too interested in findin' 'im, I guess.
And where is he now?
Well, me mate says,
The bloke I 'ave a few beers with every Friday,
He now wanders the Wannon in the west. Still takes a sheep here and there.
But he's old now. Pretty slow. And the squatters keep him in tucker.
And the ghost?

Well, he exists. Old Billy the Blacksmith's, apparently.
Got too drunk one night, slipped in and drowned.
Nobody's found 'is body, though. Funny that.
Anyway, there you have it,
The true story of 'Waltzing Matilda',
Told to me by me mate.
But a worry, isn't it? How false news can be twisted into fact?
Shows how stupid some people are,
I guess.

The Navvy – Pushing North For 'The Alice'

The first Ghan took to the rails in 1929, travelling between Adelaide and Alice Springs. The modern Ghan covers two thousand nine hundred and seventy-nine kilometres between Adelaide and Darwin.

Drag, push, hammer and sweat,
Drag, push, hammer, sweat.

His muscles are burnt by the sun,
His spiking hammer gleams like a falling star,
Sleepers rock beneath his boots,
Dog-spikes bite deep,
Rails are inching ahead

And it's
Drag, push, hammer and sweat,
Drag, push, hammer, sweat.

No mythical king, the navvy,
Cleaving the sun with a magic sword,

Rather a dusty Prometheus
Chained to the desert, his shovel, pickaxe and barrow

And it's
Drag, push, hammer and sweat,
Drag, push, hammer, sweat.

At dusk
He's a spectre rubbing its scarlet eyes
And watching the hard-edged world loosen its grip,

At night
The listener
Fixed on the looping lines of camels lamenting their loads of rails,
The clanking of bells,
The 'hooshta, hooshta' of cameleers

And,
Before the long pools of sleep draw him down,
He wants the liquid, soothing voice of his woman,
Coal black as she is,
Three hundred kilometres away in the south,
Safe in Port Augusta.

With dawn
He is again the navvy

And it's
Drag, push, hammer, sweat,
Drag, push, hammer and sweat.

Relic From the Gold Rush

In the early 1850s a peculiar madness swept through the colony of Victoria. A madness brought about by the discovery of gold. People came from all over the world to seek it. Victoria had, in 1851, a population of about 25,000. By 1861 there were over 600,000.

Clumps of yellow broom clung to the rough track
And blackberries burst from the clay slopes.
However, picking my way past the few rusty lines of fencing wire
And crazy, tilted posts,
I finally found what I had come to locate:
The carcass of an abandoned steam engine.
In front of it lay the remains of rail tracks, still as snakes in
  the long grass.
A few spikes had obviously avoided capture by curious
  souvenir hunters
And, though covered in coarse graffiti, the boiler had
  remained intact.
Bracken ferns half covered the wreck,
As if trying to conceal its shame
And I heard the dry-throated wind
And somewhere among the bushes
Bees mumbling at their work.

Stumble upon a fish wrecked on a beach
And you may still detect the echo of life,
Imagine the fish rainbow vibrant beneath the waves.
But,
Stumbling upon a wreck like this,
This relic of man's restless greed,
What can one feel?

A Winter School Day

The early 1900s, Suggan Buggan, far East Gippsland

The grey mist gathers its skirts
And trundles off into the morning.
Rust brown clouds scowl above the hills.
Kookuburras crank themselves into action
And fling their raucous laughter across the valley.
The winter sun peers through the school's single window
And spiders across the earthen floor.
Standing alone,
The teacher struggles to encourage a feeble fire
In the fireplace,
Smiles briefly as the first flames creep upwards.
Outside, harness jingles, brassy as ice.
The door creaks.
A small girl enters, prim as a new pin,
Drops her school bag,
Greets the teacher in a reed-thin voice
And moves shyly towards the fire.

The Blacksmith

Portland, 1874

The grog he shares, this Friday,
With the shambling shepherds, the surly swaggies,
The whalers, the loungers and the lost,
Is the communion wine of mateship

And, as the pains of the week slip from his shoulders,
The rapid-fire exchanges, the jostling,
The laughter, the mechanical raising of glasses,
Are the anaesthetising wine of forgetfulness.

Now, as the blurred horizon dissolves in the sea
And oppressive darkness washes through the bay,
The last loungers slouch away
And the blacksmith's drink
Becomes the communion wine of the lonely.

The Seaman and the Lighthouse

The single yellow beam scissors its way
Between the stars, peels the rind of the moon,
Catches the white, ghostly gulls as they play
And briefly makes the restless night its own,
Now seeking the edges of the known world
And now carving a trail across the sea.

Cold beneath the colourless sails already unfurled,
The sailor remembers his pointless plea,
His wife's stony face, his son's muffled tears,
The slow closing of the door, the sense
Of failure and the icy truth of years
Revealed after years of willing ignorance.

But, now, the light is frayed, a thin ribbon,
Lost, with his thoughts, on the troubled ocean.

My Father's Clock

Sixty years after he gave it to my mother,
It sits comfortably on our wall,
As compelling as any of my wife's paintings.
Its steady, mock-gold pendulum
Is the rhythmic flow of time
Taking me back to the family lounge room.
Even after all these years
It is like soothing music closing any winter's day.
Perhaps it is, for visitors, an echo from their own childhood,
An invitation to open and stop or start the pendulum.
Others might want it silenced,
See it as a door into memories they do not want to rekindle,
A childhood window they do not want to peer through.
But, for me, it is a dependable stream of connection,
A constant melody
That flows from my childhood to my eightieth year,
A door that, perhaps, when open,
Will only have meaning for me.

Revisiting an Old Wimmera Home

Spring has clearly come,
Come with the long, curled clouds,
The sheets of bright blue sky
And the skeins of copper-coloured ibises
Still landing on the dam.
But all is changed.
Gone are the uniform fields of oats and wheat,
The old, heavy-bellied trucks
And the clapped-out ploughs lined up like trophies.
All is new, space age now,
Computerised, comfortable and contained.
Wheat rubs shoulders with barley, gaudy canola,
Sorghum, millet and maize.

The track that snared my uncle's truck is sealed.
Gone are the drooping she-oaks.
Where the pigs were fed, manicured lawn now grows
And gravel paths contain disciplined garden beds.
Strangers own the farm now

And the Wimmera I knew is a memory.

Road Train Seen at Night – Southern Queensland

Used on the extensive, open roads, the longest road trains are over fifty metres in length.

You notice, at first, just the stars,
Strung together in the Milky Way,
A few wandering clouds
And the thin, metallic arc of the moon,
Now, a sliver of sound,
Now, a broadening, mysterious as thunder in a clear sky
And splashes of light parting the scattered trees,
Erratic, but coming on.

Now, you detect two yellow orbs,
Behind them, the prime mover,
The bull bar, cold, belligerently silver
And, high up, a face, staring ahead, unaware of your existence,
Finally, the three trailers,
Each with its rows of Christmas lights,
Its cramped and ghosted cattle.

Now, it is gone, plunging back into the darkness,
With its lights, its cargo to be slaughtered
And, high, distant and aloof,
The stars can again swim on,
Undisturbed through the silence of the night.

Sputnik

Built by the Soviet Union in 1957, Sputnik was the world's first satellite launch.

The old farmer smells the mown hay in the paddock,
Feels the sweat growing cold on his face
And hears, behind the rusty shed, his kelpie rattling her chain.
There is comfort in the mist trickling along the creek,
The windmill and the frogs creaking together,
The blurred outlines of cattle slouched beneath the red gum
He and his wife had planted sixty years ago,
Even in the cacophony of possums coughing in the orchard.

But tonight,
Above the sharp outline of his house
He sees, almost with disbelief,
A dot, silent, white and purposeful,
Crossing the Milky Way.

The Black Arrow: William Creek

In the 1960s, Great Britain was interested in rocket research. Four rockets were launched in the vast Australian desert. The final Black Arrow, launched in 1971, successfully put a low-level Earth satellite in orbit.

Only the sun could touch it now,
Stroke its polished thighs
And scarlet lipstick crown.
Beneath, already insignificant
In the immense nothingness of the desert,
Men seemed even more diminished.
But it was a human hand that set the rocket on its way,
Made it catapult through a flood of blinding light,
Vomit dust and flame,
Hurl unnatural thunder out over the desert,
Give birth to a satellite
And cleverly christen it *Prospero*.

But that was years ago.
Its remnants lie here, now,
Like the bloated carcass of a fish.
From its black exhaust
That scored the glassy surface of the sky
Drift spiderwebs
And what remain of its guts and Bristol engine
Are smeared with dust.

Close by,
But not too close
And pretty in her floral dress,
A child stands with her mother,
Uncertain whether to touch the corpse
Or not.

The Farmer

never nine to five

Work,
With all its monotony, its predictability
And its occasional struck spark of accomplishment,
Remains his anchor,
The practised response no longer in need of practice.

It is duty
Squaring itself against the late-night storm
As muddy boots are pulled on
And the hung coat is dragged down and hauled over shoulders
When a lamb is coughed into life on the slope above the river
And lies like a stranded jellyfish,
Shivering in its afterbirth
And watched, in its knife-edge struggle for life, by a crow.

It is the unflinching response
To the out of tune trumpet blare and sucked in breath of the beast
Steaming like an antiquated engine
And stamping in the sickly fog,
The Hereford almost ready for market, but impatient to be fed.

It is the round up
Of brown-grey Corriedales bunching together,
Grinding their teeth in summer's stifling heat
And reluctant to confront the high-pitched mechanical chatter
Within the shed.

It is the assault
On red gum trunks lying like harpooned whales
Waiting to be flensed

And with its runnels of sweat,
Its repetitive loosening and tightening of muscles
And all its fatigue,
It is a defence,
No, more a weapon
Against capitulation to the dark, tangled roots of cancer
Lurking just below his consciousness.

Visiting a Remembered Woolshed

It stands there still, an island, iron-walled, iron-roofed,
Washed by the same fleeces of flung clouds,
Slow moving shadows from the red bluff behind
And the spear-sharp sun.
But it is old, now.
The yards around it are filled with weeds,
Though the dry, concrete sheep dip, so intimidating as a child,
Still retains the lingering smell of arsenic.
Windows, robbed of glass, are gapped mouths
And the corrugated-iron tank,
Once strong as a drum, is now tilted, empty
And bleeding streams of rust.
Gone are the tides of unshorn, grey-backed sheep
And the sweeping dust.
Gone the circling dogs, eager to bark and nip,
But ears pricked and eyeing their masters.
Gone are the brown-hatted men, bustling, shoving and shouting.
The roof is a landing strip for crows
And the gravel track is lined with weeds.

It is an old man, now,
Abandoned
But perhaps content with its memories.

The Circus Tent

The circus in Australia has a long history. The first known event occurred in Sydney in 1833, given by two tightrope walkers, one of whom was a former convict. In 1847, Radford's Royal Circus opened in Tasmania. Wirth's Circus toured the country for more than a hundred years.

Having seen it there, anchored on the oval,
Billowing out like something from another world
And glittering with stars,
You felt it would remain forever.
But, of course, it hasn't.
Tucked away in the belly of a truck, it will sleep
And, then, when the time is right,
It will burst forth again, releasing its fantasies,
Its own particular realities somewhere else.
But the memories, legacies from our own childhood,
They remain:
The spangled performers,
The cavorting clowns struggling to extract a laugh,
The swimming lights,
The ball-balancing acrobats toying with gravity,
The beautiful trapeze artists flashing above our heads,
The children, willingly swept along,
The parents, bored or showing interest
And the 'oldies',
Happy, or sad,
To glimpse, in the eyes of their grandchildren,
A glimmer of their own past.

Yes. The circus has gone, now,
Settled itself briefly in some new point in Time.
But, perhaps, it will come again,
Land on our oval,
Open and rekindle those childhood memories
Once more.

The Kitchen and the Summer Storm

Lightning spears through the gullies, spills over the plain
And the mile-high columns of clouds collapse in rain.
The farmer, looks up, his hands creased as old leather.
'Shouldn't have listened to you about the weather.'
His wife, mouse-like and well versed in obedience,
Sensing he expects her to fill the spiked silence,
Offers a half smile. 'Good for our vegies, though, John.'
'Yeah. For your spuds and peas. But not for my lucerne.
Should've done my cuttin' and cartin' earlier.'
She has seen him like this before, grey as a spider,
Silent, for a time with threat, then cutting with blame.
'Rot on the ground, it will. Wives should know their place. Same
Thing happened last year.' And he goes, slamming the door,
Leaving the lightning, the rain and her guilt to gnaw
And reduce her to tears.

Through the tangle of light and dark, an ambulance,
Spitting mud from the sodden road in its advance,
Splashes away and she wonders what mishap, grave
Or fatal has occurred and who it is trying to save.

Portland: Not as I Knew it

On the fishing wharf, concrete has captured
The sea-sucking, barnacle-crusted pylons.
The bay lies, docile, tamed
And buoys mark the positions
Of a few expensive, ocean-going yachts.

Fewer are the flocks of evil-eyed, stalking gulls
That prowled the bollards, gone the salty smell
Of fish heads and the oily ribbons oozing from the hulls
Of trawlers boasting heavy catches to sell.

Now, on purpose-built promontories,
Cranes and spidering gantries stand,
Severe as mechanical mantises
Poised above impressive domes and
Snub-nosed carriers of grain.

On Battery Point, open-mouthed cannons,
Manned by vigilant sparrows,
Threaten destruction on invading Russians
And gleaming, heavy-footed 'dozers below
Labour to reshape a mountain of logs.

Freed from school, two boys
Put down their bags to admire this mastery,
Unaware that the antics of these lumbering toys
Are already seeds for a new mythology.

The Droplet

Above the font, it pauses, glows, then falls,
To set in place the naming of a child.
Its coming brings the frog and all its calls,
Those shrill poetic notes that tumble, wild

And constant through the gritty autumn air.
In spring the webs of spiders stay its end
And glow like incandescent coils of hair.
It strokes the hearts of flowers; grasses bend

And tremble as it touches, passes, leaves
A thread of sky embroidered in the green.
It hangs, complete and polished on the eaves
Of houses, takes the fading gaberdine

Of dusk and then it yields, diminutive:
A burst of colour dies that life may live.

www.ingramcontent.com/pod-product-compliance
Lightning Source LLC
Chambersburg PA
CBHW050304120526
44590CB00016B/2488